Ethics in Research

Continuum Research Methods Series

Series Editor: Richard Andrews

Action Research – Patrick Costello

Analysing Media Texts – Andrew Burn and David Parker

Evaluation Methods in Research – Judith Bennett

Research Questions – Richard Andrews

Researching Post-Compulsory Education – Jill Jameson and
  Yvonne Hillier

Systematic Reviews – Carole Torgerson

Using Focus Groups in Research – Lia Litosseliti

Real World Research Series

Series Editor: Bill Gillham

Case Study in Research Methods – Bill Gillham

Developing a Questionnaire – Bill Gillham

The Research Interview – Bill Gillham

Ethics in Research

Ian Gregory

continuum
LONDON • NEW YORK

Continuum

The Tower Building
11 York Road
London SE1 7NX

15th East 26th Street
New York
NY 10010

British Library Cataloguing-in-Publication Data
A catalogue record for this book is available from the British Library.

ISBN 0–8264–6477–7 (paperback) SmC 610.7₂ GRE

Typeset by YHT Ltd, London
Printed and bound in Great Britain by MPG Books Ltd, Bodmin, Cornwall

To Julia, Tessa, Lydia, Tom and Ben
They deserve so much better

Contents

Series Editor's Introduction ix

Preface xi

Introduction 1

1 Reflections on the Idea of Research 5

2 Social and Educational Research – At Last 17

3 Ethics and the Research Question 27

4 The Principle of Consent 35

5 On Confidentiality 49

6 Further Issues about Consent 59

7 Moral Issues in Research 67

Recommended Further Reading 79

Series Editor's Introduction

The Continuum Research Methods series aims to provide undergraduate, Masters and research students with accessible and authoritative guides to particular aspects of research methodology. Each title looks specifically at one topic and gives it in-depth treatment, very much in the tradition of the Rediguide series of the 1960s and 1970s.

Such an approach allows students to choose the books that are most appropriate to their own projects, whether they are working on a short dissertation, a medium-length work (15–40 000 words) or a fully-fledged thesis at MPhil or PhD level. Each title includes examples of students' work, clear explication of the principles and practices involved, and summaries of how best to check that your research is on course.

In due course, individual titles will be combined into larger books and, subsequently, into encyclopaedic works for reference.

The series will also be of use to researchers designing funded projects, and to supervisors who wish to recommend in-depth help to their research students.

Richard Andrews

Preface

This is a highly selective look at some themes arising from a concern with the ethics of research. It pays more attention than might be normal to the idea of research itself. I seek to emphasize the importance of integrity, both intellectual and moral, as holding the key to the best research can be. The discussion of the specifically moral dimensions of research is too sketchy to be wholly satisfactory. The hope is that further and deeper thought on the issues broached might be encouraged.

Introduction

This is a short book on a large and (extremely) complex topic: the ethical dimensions of research involving human subjects. Like other books in this series, it is primarily addressed to what I will call 'tiros' in research matters. A tiro is a beginner, an individual learning his or her craft. For our purposes, this means students in the foothills of mastering the skills of being a good social and educational researcher. More specifically, it denotes third-year undergraduates, MA students, and doctoral candidates who have to satisfy their respective examiners that they can do a decent piece of research. Both the length of the book and the intended audience mean a concentration on some topics rather than others. Methodological matters are methodological matters are methodological matters. That is to say, they apply indifferently to whoever is doing a certain kind of research, irrespective of at what stage in their research careers they might be. If a questionnaire is being devised, certain canons of construction have to be satisfied if it is to serve its purpose. If interview materials are being analysed, then certain procedures should be gone through.

It seems to me that ethical concerns impact differently at different stages of a researcher's career. In the case of the ethics of research, some issues that might confront the funded researcher about his relationship to those providing the funding and the uses to which they might put his findings, do not seem live issues for final-year undergraduates, given the usual circumstances of their research. For that reason, this text concentrates on those issues which are common to all researchers rather than those more peculiar to more established practitioners of the art of human research. None of this is to suggest that the problems not pursued are unimportant. It is simply to recognize that addressing all of the issues of the ethics of human research would call for an altogether more ambitious piece of writing. No doubt many of those still in the foothills of their careers as researchers aspire to joining the world of those whose professional lives in large measure consist of doing research – either as academics, or as the recipients of money from foundations who fund approved research. At that stage, some of the problems barely mentioned here will become of more pressing significance for them.

The ethics of educational and social research embraces moral issues arising out of the conduct of research. For our purposes, the terms 'ethical' and 'moral' will be used interchangeably. If there is ever any point in distinguishing between the ethical and the moral, between ethical and moral commitments, between ethical and moral codes, the concerns of this text are not that occasion. The writer will be satisfied if at the end the reader is a little more sensitive to the problematic issues surrounding 'the ethics of research'. The approach to these concerns will be philosophical in tone; *in tone* because while very fundamental issues are raised, the treatment is a little too cursory to qualify as sternly philosophical. I write this from the perspective of one who believes that the best philosophy is analytical in tone and distinguished by its unrelenting and rigorous argument. The ambitions of this text will hopefully repay a more impressionistic style of writing.

This book will be different from some others in the series in that it is not in the business of providing answers to moral concerns researchers might have. In the end, the researcher has to accept responsibility for the resolution of moral perplexities. Advice may be sought from others, and given. Others cannot make moral decisions on a researcher's behalf. The writer adopts a protestant attitude towards the confronting of ethical issues. What passes muster as ethically responsible research is down to the individual researcher and no one else. Judgement has to be exercised when deciding how the researcher ought to conduct him or herself if faced with significant moral choices during the research process. Judgements made are inescapably personal if moral in kind. The character of the researcher is crucial in shaping the outcomes of moral deliberations as they arise in social and educational research. But the processes and considerations involved in the making of such moral decisions can be better exercised, and decisions made grounded in properly relevant considerations. This book is directed to the encouragement of these possibilities.

An initial point that maybe does not need making but which, nevertheless, I will make: I take it as read that through the exercise of reason and critical enquiry we can get closer to knowing the truth of things, can come to know and understand better than we did previously. Nobody imagines it is easy to dispel error and confusion. The penetration of the veil of ignorance demands all our cognitive and imaginative resources. Getting closer to knowing and understanding 'how and why things are as they are' is certainly an arduous and endless enterprise. Whatever the area of intellectual concern and activity, there are narratives that make better sense of things for the simple reason that they are more true and less error-ridden than alternative accounts. There really are things 'out there' to be accurately described and understood.

The very idea of research is barely coherent unless we accept such a proposition. Whether we come to know and understand is down to us – so far we have not done badly. What we come to know is determined by how the world is. We have to start somewhere, and the commitment to objective states of affairs we strive to understand, and can come to understand, is the beginning point of this text.

I take it as read throughout the text that researchers are familiar with, and act in accordance with, legal requirements relevant to their research interests and concerns. Certainly what the law demands or forbids is, fairly typically, seen as part of any moral equation touching considerations as to how we should act. Researchers should conduct themselves at all times in a manner consonant with the law.

The discussion is general. There are many different kinds of social and educational research. I leave it to the researcher to translate any broad directives found in the text, suggested as pertinent to what they ought to do *qua* researcher, into action appropriate to their kind of research.

1

Reflections on the Idea of Research

Huge amounts of what we have come to know and understand is the product of research. The activity of educating individuals, to a great degree represents the effort, individual and collective, to pass on what it is we have come to know and understand, along with something of the ways in which the various kinds of knowledge and understanding we now possess have been won. One of our concerns is with the so called 'ethics of educational research', where educational research is that research designed to cast light upon the myriad of problems arising from the effort to educate. Before looking directly at the ethical issues that will concern us, it might be as well to spend some time looking at the very idea of research. We will remind ourselves how commonplace the conduct of research is, but how the natural activity of researching can be professionalized and institutionalized so as to be the driving force behind the extraordinary accomplishments of humankind in making sense of the world (physical and social) in which we live. And we will come to see how social and educational research is part of the sustained effort to understand better than we do now the nature of social and educational phenomena.

The *Shorter Oxford English Dictionary* defines research as follows: (1) the action or an instance of searching carefully for a specified thing or person ... (2) a search or investigation undertaken to discover facts and reach new conclusions by the critical study of a subject or by a course of scientific inquiry ... (3) systematic investigation into and study of materials, sources etc to establish facts, collate information.... . Putting it shortly, research is a species of finding things out. To talk of it in these terms is simply to highlight that not all instances of finding things out are the result of research. We not only can, but do, find things out owing nothing to research. We can find things out wholly by chance, accidentally, with no great effort. I might find out my wife is having an affair by overhearing a conversation, by capturing her in flagrante with her lover when returning home two days early from a trip abroad. I might read in the paper that Australia have beaten us again at cricket despite only buying the paper to find out what time *Eastenders* is on the television. Neither the knowledge we have lost again at cricket or finding out *Eastenders* is at 7.30pm and not 8.00pm is the product of research. Gossip, malicious rumour, eavesdropping on private conversations, hacking into someone's computer as well as loftier activities such as reading an item in a quality newspaper on the spread of Aids and its incidence, watching a popular arts or science programme on the television or radio or going to the dictionary to look up the meaning of a word can all be sources of information, allowing us to find out things that otherwise we might not know. There is no need to belabour the point. I doubt if it is possible to list all the sources available to us that put us in the way of information that might prompt us to say to another 'Guess what I have just found out.' In our lifetimes, and throughout our lifetimes, we find things out all the time. 'Finding out' here means not much more than that we come to know things about the world (natural, political and social), about other people's affairs and concerns, partialities and proclivities, accomplishments and achievements, that failing exposure to these avenues of information we might not otherwise know. A lot of what we find out, as we put it, might transpire not to be true at all: if you like, we are mistaken in thinking we have found something out. But finding out the truth of things about which we are mistaken is itself often very easily put right. We realize we have misheard what another was saying, we read an apology in a paper for its misrepresentation of the facts to which we have given such credence, and so on.

In many instances of coming to know and understand, it will not always be clear whether our knowing and understanding are the outcomes of research or simply finding out. Different individuals will be inclined to use one form of words rather than another. And nothing of substance will turn on how we speak. There will be clear instances of finding out – pure and simple as it were – and clear instances of research having been undertaken that has given a knowledge and understanding, a degree of insight which only research could have delivered. I have given instances of the former in the last paragraph. We can all think of instances of research with a big R, as it were. The interesting questions are whether there are any general features that seem to define what it is unproblematically 'to do research', whether such a characterization has any implications for the topic of this text: ethics and research.

The first point to cling on to is that there are as many kinds of research as there are kinds of things to find out about. We can all think of, and list, instances of research across the whole gamut of human concerns and interests. Just look at any university prospectus with its list of departments academics, research fellows and students within those departments: in all of those departments research will be conducted. The Research Assessment Exercise, to which so much time is devoted and in the light of which the financial well-being of British universities is determined, represents an effort to pass judgement on the quality of that research while at the same time being indicative of the variety of that research effort. Even allowing for a distinction between research universities and teaching universities, it is a pardonable exaggeration to say that every academic will (in some guise) see him or herself as a researcher, as will many students, certainly for part of the time.

We need not to be too prescriptive about what we are prepared to count as research. To say that only academics, or academics of a certain sort, do research is obviously to fail to do justice to those many other individuals who do exactly the kind of thing that passes as research in the universities, but in some other context which is not university-based. There are many research institutes quite separate from universities which nevertheless, peopled as they are by individuals with similar educational backgrounds and qualifications, unambiguously do research. More importantly, however, research in a quite unremarkable sense can be done by those who lack all those qualifications, who may not even be in pursuit of such qualifications. And clearly research is done by those aspiring to such qualifications but not yet possessing them. Research, in short, is not a matter of qualifications. What distinguishes research (perhaps, distinct from being a researcher with a big R) is how individuals *set about* finding out what it is they wish to find out, and also something about why it is they want to find out what they are bent on finding out.

Let me unpack these very bare comments. I have already made the point that many things can be found out by accident, without any effort, purely incidentally: one as it were, 'comes by' what is found out. Whatever research is, it represents an effort to find some things out. To research something, whatever it might be and whatever the context, is to take upon oneself responsibility for the task of determining some fact or facts, clarifying some issue, understanding better in the light of the research undertaken something only dimly understood before, and so on. Using the language previously italicized the person researching sets about finding something out. There is a purposive, more systematic dimension to that kind of finding out that we are tempted to think of as research. The context and the ambitions of the research can be more or less lofty. Research into a cure for Aids has momentous implications; research into the history of the local village football team less so. Research into Aids breaks down into a series of research endeavours conducted by well-funded teams of researchers exploring different dimensions of the illness, its causation and manifestations; research into the history of the local village football team may involve one enthusiast taking advantage of any spare time he has to pursue his interest. The successful outcomes of research may have profound implications for many, or simply the satisfaction afforded the individual researcher following (as he deems it) the successful outcomes of his research endeavours. Not all research need (even if carried through successfully) come up with something new. Much research – it all depends who does it – revisits the already familiar and established, and confirms what is familiar and established.

The motivation behind research can be extraordinarily various: just to show you can do it, to get an MA, to show you are as bright as the next person, because you are impelled to do it, as part of the effort to change the world, for its own sake, because you want to get on in the world, because it has to be done, to attract the admiration of the girl next door, to keep your job, to not let your colleagues down, to be in a position to damage another's reputation, and so on. The motivation to engage in a piece of research can range from the noblest of motives to the downright base. It is most unclear if there are any very general comments to be made about the nature of research itself except the following: if research is seriously undertaken (as against going *through the motions* of researching or playing at doing research) there is involved a systematic, purposive effort at finding something out with a view to being clearer about the object you are striving to find out about.

Serious Research

Research, understood as the activity of more systematically trying to find something out (whatever that something might be), is an undertaking distinctive of our species. Our curiosity demands satisfaction and commonly we seek to satisfy that curiosity by undertaking research. We should see research with a big R as a continuation of what goes on in our everyday lives. Researchers (with a big R) concern themselves with the issues engaging their interest in a more serious and self-reflective manner than is normally the case when we are conducting an investigation designed to cast light on some more mundane state of affairs – where does my morning paper disappear to every morning, why does Jane so dislike me? The sense of seriousness often flows from a sense that the problems being addressed have a weight and importance not associated with so much of our everyday lives. The weight and importance of these issues have significance not because they are necessarily of great moment to our ordinary lives, but rather because fellow practitioners of that kind of research recognize them as crucial to the understanding of issues a given discipline exists to promote. And it is because Researchers see themselves as part of a larger endeavour to

understand which they share with their fellow researchers, that they are that much more self-conscious about the
nature of what they are doing. They feel the need to be
aware of other research in their area of concern, they are
conscious of what constitutes the appropriate way of
conducting the research into the questions they are
interested in, and they know they will have to satisfy the
critical eye of their fellow researchers.

This will certainly involve some kind of reporting to
that body of expert research opinion on their own
research. The canons of research that must be satisfied
will, of course, vary according to the nature of the questions being investigated. In our times, most researchers
concentrate their efforts on a narrow range of related
issues. Division of labour is as much a feature of intellectual life as it is in any other area of human life. Nowadays, it is a very rare bird indeed who contributes through
their research efforts to more than one narrow region of
the research enterprise. Not all research is equally
momentous or as valued. Within the universe of the
professional researcher there is a recognition that some
research is of fundamental significance, some is run of
the mill, and some is barely worth the doing. Some
researchers have insights denied to the rest of us, some
trudge along as worthy under-labourers living off the
work of others, and some (perfectly justifiably) will forever be unheralded. But uniting all of them and all of
their efforts is that systematic and purposive effort to
know and understand something better than they did
prior to the research.

Research in its professional and institutionalized guise
is energized by a sense of the importance of knowing and
understanding. The desire to know and understand better and more completely than we presently do is forever
with us, and research is the vehicle through which we
achieve that deeper understanding. While individual

motivation to do a certain piece of research may have its genesis in all kinds of considerations, for example, trying to achieve promotion, putting someone in their place, settling old scores, making parents proud – the list could go on and on – it seems reasonable to recognize that in response to the question of what justifies (rather than explains) the research undertaken the following might be claimed: any knowledge and understanding gleaned is self-justifying (is valuable in itself, worth doing for its own sake); the knowledge and understanding flowing from the research undertaken allows us to do things, achieve ends, that otherwise we could not do; and what we know and understand as a consequence of research allows us to make the world a better place than it was before – we can replace misery and privation with a degree of happiness and well-being that would otherwise not be possible.

No doubt each of these responses seems more plausible in some contexts rather than in others. Justifying a piece of recondite philosophical research into ontology by appealing to its being worth doing for its own sake is more plausible than claiming it will shape for the better the world within which we pass our lives. Research into engineering problems to do with the putting up of bridges looks a likely candidate for justification in terms of what we can now do that we might not have been able to do before. And research into the impact of gender issues on career choices might easily seek to vindicate itself through the way findings might impact upon (say) educational and social policies governing the allocation of career possibilities for the population at large. Be all of that as it may, it is not uncommon for all of these responses to be invoked in justifying some research being undertaken. After all, most of us feel the pull of these distinctive forms of justification. It is easy to be impressed by knowledge and understanding that allows us to do things we previously could not. It is uplifting to be reassured that knowledge and understanding can aid us in discharging our sense of moral obligation towards others who are, perhaps, less fortunate than ourselves. It is suitably high-minded to recognize that the pursuit of knowledge and understanding has a claim upon our allegiance irrespective of its payoff in other terms. But underlying each and all these characteristic responses is that enhanced comprehension of how things are (to use a portmanteau phrase) which Research has enabled. The pursuit of knowledge and understanding is the supreme imperative underlying Research. In large part, all the ethical dilemmas arising from the Research effort stem from the claims of Research to achieve more extensive and deeper levels of knowing and understanding. More of this later.

It is important to grasp how constraining of the activities of the Researcher the ends of knowing and understanding are, how the achieving of deeper insights makes demands of Researchers that must be satisfied. Anyone (Researcher or not) researching anything has to bow to the demands incumbent upon them *qua* researcher. Knowledge and understanding, being possessed of new insights, appreciating more discriminatingly (and all such ends) do not come easily. Anyone who sets themselves to find out something in a systematic and purposive manner is familiar with how arduous (physically and personally) the conduct of research can be. No doubt all research might be done better, more sensitively, than it is. Much research has evident flaws. We do talk of pieces of research as being 'deeply flawed'. There will be instances in which the research is so deeply flawed we feel justified in refusing the product the honorific title 'research'. There are, however, many cases where we feel that while the research has failings, nevertheless we do see it as part of a research effort. There might be a failure to deliver adequately on the impersonal demands which any research worth the name must strive to recognize. The failure, however, is a failure of delivery rather than a failure to take seriously the demands intrinsic to the conduct of any research worth the name. The difference between research seriously undertaken and that which we are not prepared to countenance as research lies precisely in whether the constraints that the pursuit of knowledge and understanding impose upon us have been given due and proper weight.

But what are the imperatives that the conduct of research demands be met? We expect anything that passes as research to have a certain *integrity*. We characteristically commend people for their integrity, even if on occasion we find their integrity irksome, standing as it does in the way of the realizing of our own schemes. The notion of integrity itself demands much unpacking, but for our purposes the following will suffice: Integrity finds its natural home within a context in which there is a recognition that certain principles (of action, of style and composition, of sportsmanship etc.) demand to be satisfied and where no matter what the temptations to disregard those principles, an individual clings hard to them in what they do. 'If I am to be true to myself, I can do no other' is the somewhat clichéd response associated with those demonstrating moral integrity. Analogously in the research domain, if a research text possesses integrity, it does so because the researchers, conscious of the demands of the conduct of research, strive as hard as they can to ensure that those demands are satisfied. What is intolerable in respect of research is the deliberate disregard of the canons governing the conduct of research. Research is driven by the desire to advance knowledge and understanding (on our own part, and, if we are lucky, on behalf of others). The very purpose of research, at the more mundane as well as the loftier levels of research activity, can only be served by taking seriously certain intellectual demands intrinsic to the advancement of knowledge and understanding.

The motivation behind the research enterprise can be extraordinarily diverse, as previously mentioned, ranging from the noble to the most base. But the conduct of the research itself has to be subject to the practice of the intellectual and moral habits intrinsic to the conduct of research. None of the habits of mind we expect to see satisfied in the conduct of research occasions any surprise when we see them listed. But the actual practice of such habits of mind can be demanding in the extreme – and the more so if we are researching something with a view to advancing our own ends and prospects. To realize that what we might wish to be the case is not going to transpire poses temptations that can be hard to resist. The falsification of research to advance private and partial ends is far too familiar a feature of our intellectual and human story for us not to recognize how burdensome the demands of intellectual integrity can sometimes be. Research is an *epistemic* enterprise and as such must strive to satisfy those dictates of reason which best put us in a position to achieve levels of (cognitive) awareness that might otherwise be denied us. All subsequent remarks are now addressed to the kinds of research universities exist to promote and encourage. It is in such a context we can better see writ large the demands research, seriously undertaken, must satisfy.

Individuals are perplexed by problems (supply your own example). They want to find some answer or answers to those perplexities. In solving one problem, they might be left with further and (perhaps) even greater questions crying out for answers. But it is enough to be going with that a present perplexity is better understood. At the most general level we can say the following: Researchers need to be as clear as they can be just what their problem is. According to the issue to be explored, the researcher needs to engage in the mode of enquiry appropriate to the kind of issue it is that is causing intellectual discomfort or posing an intellectual challenge. Mathematical problems are broached in their own distinctive manner; trying to understand the past poses its own peculiar challenges captured by the practice of historians; the physicist typically sets about dealing with his or her concerns in the ways sanctioned by the community of physical scientists; the literary critic seeks appreciation in one or other of the ways countenanced by the practice of literary criticism, and so on. These methodologies – for this is what they are – generate the data, provide the evidence, that will enable the researcher to start to understand the issue or issues that gave impetus to the research in the first place. In the event of a researcher claiming an enhanced appreciation of 'how things are,' he or she seeks to justify the claims made by showing how conclusions drawn are vindicated by the data generated. If their fellow practitioners and researchers are persuaded by the claims made – because some pattern of reasoning typifying successful research in that area is fully exemplified – the research will be deemed a success. It will not, of course, be the last word, but something has been found out, and in a manner satisfying the dictates of reason.

2

Social and Educational Research – At Last

How do these very general, highly programmatic observations translate into the idiom of social and educational research? Rather baldly, it will be taken for granted that educational research is the systematic and purposive effort to contribute to a better understanding than we presently possess on how to deliver upon all those ambitions associated with the tasks of education. Education is a moral enterprise through which we seek the transformation of lives by initiating individuals into the cultural achievements of humanity. Education is a key element in allowing human beings to realise the potentialities they all possess. The content of educational programmes is geared to promoting and encouraging the development of the extraordinarily diverse range of talents and skills and accomplishments of which humans are capable. While the overwhelming thrust of what is to come in the rest of this text is directed to educational research as an empirical enterprise, as one of the human sciences, it is as well, however, to mention at this stage that there always exists the attendant risk the educational researcher bent upon researching some issue in the here and now might fail to raise his or her eyes and ask the question 'Is what we are presently aspiring to what we ought to be aspiring to, is this really what education should be about?' If we are starting to engage more directly with the subject matter of ethics and educational research, the *educational* researcher should always remember the commitment, not only to the proper conduct of research, but also to education – the only benign avenue open to us to transmit those values and valuable enterprises that can so uplift and transform individual lives. How such a commitment should inform the lives of individual researchers raises issues demanding another book.

All the formal and informal avenues for advancing educational ends are part of (and only a very small part of) the social world which is the object of study of the social sciences. Anything said from now on will apply indifferently to the more particular world of educational research, and to social scientific research more generally.

Research that is clear as to the issues to be explored is always likely to be more successful than that which is confused as to its ambitions. This is not to say that confused research might not be stimulating of valuable future research or that its very confusions might not point the way forward for other researchers. Clear research ambitions do however maximize their chances of being successful. Wittgenstein says something to the effect that in pssychology (which we can generalize to the human sciences) there is empirical method and conceptual confusion. What I take this to (in part) mean is that if the way in which a problem is framed is lacking in clarity because the language used is systematically ambiguous between different possibilities of meaning, the collection of data can be infected in various ways. Lacking clarity as to the problem posed, the wrong data is collected, or it is difficult to make sense of data collected given the lack of certainty as to the meanings of key concepts. Unless you collect data relevant to the research issue, the research is likely to be deeply, and perhaps fatally, flawed. You can be as rigorous as you like in your empirical method but if that effort is simply ill- or mis-directed, it is wasted effort.

Trying to formulate your research questions as clearly as you can forces you to address the issue of just what it is you want to understand better. Defining key terms can either be a matter of capturing the essential and descriptive meaning of a term, or of stipulating what you for the purposes of the research will take it to mean ('By "class" I will mean …'). Clarity, however achieved, should be the goal informing the articulation of research problems.

Settling upon your research questions and being clear as to their substance is crucial to so much else that follows: the research techniques used for the eliciting of data, what data is germane to your concerns. The significance of your data has then to be assessed. It has (let us call it) an intrinsic significance. Taken on its own, what does your data suggest is or is not the case? It further possesses, by way of contrast, an extrinsic significance. This can be discerned by relating your own findings to other research that seems to bear upon your concerns. This allows us to see whether your findings are of a piece (or not) with other work done in the area. Anything aspiring to scientific standing needs to be subject to the judgement of the larger community of researchers and scholars. All of this demands considerable intellectual rigour and subtlety, which will certainly not be forthcoming unless rooted in a serious engagement with the canons of research. The element looming largest as evidence of a proper commitment to those dictates of research lies in trying to satisfy the requirements relating to drawing appropriate inferences and conclusions in the light of the evidence. To this end, the honest researcher tries to ensure that claims to greater knowledge and understanding can be sustained. The validation of this claimed-for understanding is that others in the field, familiar with the patterns of reasoning that define an area of intellectual concern, are prepared to concede that the conventions governing good reasoning in respect of a given kind of problem have been satisfied.

To this end, the researcher must be meticulous in the gathering of relevant data. To this end, the researcher must strive as hard as possible to be true to the implications of the data. If the best reading of the data is indeterminate in its significances (internal and external) this should be made plain. If the data is uncongenial to the researcher, this displeasing reality must be embraced, even if not happily. There can be no question of falsifying data to come to conclusions more in accord with your preferences as to how things are or ought to be. There must be no deliberately ignoring quotes or facts you recognize as inconvenient. The methodological maxim 'Look for negative instances', when taken seriously, encourages the idea that we must follow where the research takes us. Intellectual sleight of hand of any kind stands condemned in terms of the integrity of the research enterprise. It is poor research, and the lack of (intellectual) principle informing the research draws moral condemnation. It is, putting it shortly, a form of cheating – a term of moral opprobrium, if any is.

Research (serious enquiry) aims at truth. It can be more or less successful in that ambition, can get close to or fall far short of what it seeks to achieve. Sometimes just trying to establish 'the facts of the situation' as we put it can be very difficult. The world (physical or social) inconveniently does not always (or even often) open itself up so easily to our gaze. The unamenability of the world to our efforts to lay bare its secrets can challenge us to the very limits of our human capacities to know and understand. It is a kind of tribute to humankind that we have achieved as much as we have in terms of knowing and understanding. Another set of barriers that make finding out so hard for us, however, can be those attributable not to the world but to ourselves. Humans are prone to self-deception, to being unduly attached to individuals or causes, to wishful thinking, all of which can get in the way of a proper and realistic appreciation of the truth of affairs.

The internal and external obstacles too briefly noted above hinder our efforts to be true, both to ourselves and to the facts. The attachment to the importance of truth, being better informed, having a preference for knowledge and understanding rather than comfortable myths and half truths needs to be strong and operative in our outlook if we are to overcome our natural human tendencies. The ideals of truth, knowledge, understanding and the celebration of reason in human affairs are demanding and not at all easy to satisfy. But the burdens they impose upon us must be discharged if we are to make a better sense of the world (both physical and social) within which we pass our lives. The task of all researchers is to measure up to those demands. Realistically, we should recognize that the inspiration to be derived from high sounding notions like truth, reason, knowledge and understanding, while motivating some of our greatest accomplishments, is at best a necessary condition of research achieving its goals. In whatever area of research we are engaged, certain characteristics are needed to complement these lofty ideals. We need more to sustain us than the attachment to truth as we aim at uncovering truth or advancing our knowledge of recondite fact or achieving a deeper understanding of something.

This is a very murky area. We have already seen that certain intellectual canons that flow from the very cause of truth and understanding must be met. In particular, there must be a scrupulous attention to eliciting relevant data and drawing conclusions from that data that stand up to the critical gaze of peers in the area. Being careful as to the conclusions drawn, only claiming what the evidence supports, is the overriding intellectual virtue. Conducting one's research in accordance with the appropriate canons of reasoning maximizes the generation of the data needed to cast possible light upon the research concern. Formulating the research questions to direct the search for the sought-after data is of the essence to good research. There is no doubt some are more driven by such intellectual attachments than others, and by that token are likely to be better and more successful researchers. Allied to their natural intellectual gifts, they may make more of a mark upon the world of research. We have noted that individuals can fall short of even their best ambitions in these regards because of being self-deceiving, because of strong ideological convictions, because of being prone to wishful thinking. And we have noted how research could deliberately be falsified to serve ulterior purposes. All of these kinds of considerations speak to the character of the researcher. Coming to the heart of the matter, it seems entirely unrealistic to suppose that the confrontation of ethical issues in any kind of research, let alone educational and social research, would not in very important ways be influenced by the character of the researcher.

Individuals reveal their characters through their actions. In the light of how they behave we can infer dispositions of various kinds (where a disposition can be defined as a tendency to act in certain ways in certain situations). Someone who is irascible is a person who in his dealings with others typically exhibits irritation and is easily moved to anger. Individuals are of a generous disposition if typically they deal with others in a kindly manner and try to help them if they can. Michelle is courageous if despite the pain she continually feels, she soldiers on pursuing the goals she has set herself. And so on. Someone's character is an amalgam or constellation of those dispositions (good and bad) which constitute their personality. And, of course, we frequently arrive at an overall judgement of a person's character through being impressed by a certain mix of dispositions we deem them to have. Mary is a young woman of the highest moral character (she always tells the truth, is chaste, goes out of her way to help others); Louise seems to us to be of a doubtful moral character (she lies too easily, treats her parents with contempt, is conducting an affair while married). In this context, we talk easily of virtues and vices. The virtue of honesty lies in the disposition to tell the truth, whenever. The vice of dilatoriness lies in the disposition of always delaying what ought to be done now. Researchers bring to the conduct of research the characters they have, and certainly it can only be expected that the confronting of those moral issues they are likely to meet in the conduct of research must be significantly influenced by their moral character.

We will return to all of this in a little while. For the sake of completeness, attention is drawn to how very complicated the relationship of epistemological commitments, (those dedicated to truth, knowledge and understanding) to other personality features can be. Some (not I suspect very many) are so inspired by the ideal of truth that they exhibit in its pursuit extraordinary courage, take extreme risks, put themselves to every inconvenience in its pursuit. They try the (dangerous) drug out on themselves rather than on another. They expose themselves to great danger in order to establish the existence of a very rare plant in a dangerous ravine. Despite their phobia about flying, they take a plane to a conference at the other end of the world to confront their critics. The perceived claim upon them of getting something right, finding something out, drives such individuals on.

For the rest of us, the seriousness with which we seek insight and deeper comprehension of the object of our research is typically much less heroic, but still interestingly revelatory. Almost all research that engages those in universities and similar institutions has prolonged periods of great tedium which really do challenge our commitment to doing the research properly. Some research is exciting, but much is mundane and calls upon us to demonstrate a certain epistemological virtue. Every student doing a piece of educational research involving interviews quickly appreciates the grinding dreariness and humdrum quality of transcribing interview materials. Acre upon acre of words demanding transcription in longhand, the long business of reading and poring over such materials in the hope of an interesting quote, wading through a mass of material that is too often simply irrelevant. Such experiences call upon a certain determination to see things through, persistence and diligence, an ability to stick to the task rather than going out with your friends.

A great deal of the time devoted to research is simply dispiriting. You seem to be getting nowhere. You ask yourself if it is really worth the effort, when everything you seem to be finding out is so unexciting, merely confirmatory of what you already know. The temptation to cut corners, to tweak quotes to make them more interesting, both in expression and in their substance, can be very strong. After all, it really is highly unlikely that your examiner will actually ask to see your original data with a view to checking the accuracy and authenticity of your quotes. And what is true of transcribing quotes typifies a great deal of what goes on across the variety of techniques used to elicit data in the pursuit of research. Yet another day in the classroom observing 7-year-olds struggling with the new maths scheme and then having to go home and impose order upon the observations made, thereby yet again having to miss your favourite TV programme. To see research through to a successful conclusion involves, for most of us a great deal of the time, having to draw upon personal resources that allow us to resist the temptation to be doing other things, that allow us to somehow come to terms with the routinized nature of so much of what we are having to do. If we did not have such capacities, the research would not get done. And, of course, in many instances it does not.

The reality is that some are so driven by zeal for the truth that they are not seized by tedium in the same way as the rest of us. Some are so motivated by the thought of personal advancement, establishing a reputation, getting a first, they too are less affected by the ordinariness of what they are doing. For many of the rest of us, that we persist with our research is a tribute to the kind of individuals we are. Virtue, in a sense, enjoys its own reward. We complete the research. We understand a little better than we did. We establish a useful fact or two. We might even make a small contribution to other people's understanding of an issue, and we note with pleasure that they are grateful to us. It was hard work, but it was hard work that says something about us as individuals. In the end we have preserved and demonstrated our integrity. And, arguably, we have in small ways expressed both intellectual integrity and a certain moral integrity – we were not prepared to cheat ourselves or others. The more researchers act like this, the more certain consumers of research are that fellow researchers are clinging hard to intellectual and moral integrity, and the greater trust there can be in the products of research. Many of the attributes we demonstrate in bringing the research to a successful conclusion are admirable. They go to the very heart of who we are, and along with other more obviously moral motivations will influence how we deal with the inescapable moral quandaries the conduct of educational research throws up. It is now time to turn to the different dimensions of ethical concern informing such research.

3

Ethics and the Research Question

Educational research, in particular, has as its overriding goal a more profound knowledge and understanding of what is happening in those institutions whose task it is to deliver education. All educational research worth the name is distinguished by its recognizable interest in laying bare to our gaze an aspect (no matter how small or limited) of that most momentous of human tasks: the provision of education. We want to know where we are failing, and why we are failing. We want to know where we are succeeding, and why this is so. The vindication of educational research is in its impact upon practice. The key role of educational research is pursuing in a systematic manner, the truth about what is going on in our schools and universities as they take on the task of educating future generations. More generally, the social sciences strive to understand all manner of areas of human activity, practices, cultures and conventions. At this stage in the development of the social sciences, there will be very few areas of human life in all of its extraordinary diversity and variety that have not been exposed to the scrutinizing eye of the social scientist. And significant amounts of such activity have been driven by the desire to make a difference in some way, on the basis of a better understanding of the object of research.

Human beings, their interests and concerns, lie at the

very heart of the world of the researcher. Given that it is human beings who are to be exposed to the research endeavour, we do well to remain sensitive to the morally-laden nature of our dealings with one another. So much of the time we live our lives at a fairly unreflective level, living comfortably in accordance with established convention. Most of our lives, most of the time, we do not feel assailed by moral issues arising from the conduct of everyday life. Morality is a social mechanism that allows things human to go better than otherwise they might. The stuff of morality is a mix of character traits, sentiments, and attachment to ideals, principles and rules of behaviour promoting, and protective of, the interests of other humans. Morality acts as a constraint upon the unconstrained pursuit of our own private wants and ambitions. Morality stands as a reminder that the hopes and ambitions of others, their interests and concerns, have a claim upon us when we are thinking about what to do. What we want to do is often in opposition to what we ought to do. And what we ought to do is often of matter of what morality requires. Morality gives us good reasons to act in one way rather than another. There are many things we are morally permitted to do. But there are occasions when either (negatively) we should not harm others (damage or frustrate their interests) and other occasions when (positively) we should benefit others (promote their interests and concerns). What is true more generally can be true of situations that can confront the researcher going about his or her task. Let's explore a little how ethical concerns can touch the different stages of research.

There is more than one way to conceptualize the research process. For our purposes, it will suffice to (rather arbitrarily) draw lines between

- Deciding what to research

- Setting the research up
- Conducting the research
- Bringing the research to its conclusion.

Deciding what to research

There is no more important part of the conduct of a piece of empirical research than settling on the question or questions that will be the focal point of your research – the issues you wish to understand better as a consequence of the research undertaken. This will be absolutely crucial in directing your attention to one set of concerns rather than another. It will determine which data to elicit, which in turn will have an important influence upon which research strategy is pursued. Providing you have formulated your question with clarity, gained access to appropriate data and familiarized yourself with other reported relevant research, you have maximized your chances of producing a decent report of the research. As mentioned before, even if the elements of a good piece of research are in place, the researcher will still have to satisfy the epistemological canons which the serious pursuit of truth demands be satisfied. Pre-eminently among these canons is that the evidence supports conclusions drawn.

The determination of the research question normally generates little in the way of moral concern. After what seems (is) a lifetime of supervising students doing research at all levels I can scarcely recall an instance in which the very topic chosen for research made me have anxieties about the moral appropriateness of the piece of research proposed. But consider the following scenario not far removed from one that arose recently. A female undergraduate was interested in researching issues to do with the impact of eating disorders among young adolescent girls upon their school experience. To this end, it was proposed she might go into a local school and interview a sample of young female students on what they thought about eating disorders and whether they had thoughts (either from personal experience or derived from someone they knew suffering from such a disorder) about how eating disorders touched school lives. Additionally, it was mooted there might be some exploration of how far, if at all, the school recognized the existence of such problems and whether, in the light of such a recognition, it put into place mechanisms and policies designed to alleviate the impact eating disorders had on young lives within the school. There is no doubt that there are significant numbers of young people who are badly affected by eating disorders. There cannot be any serious doubt that problems in eating may well affect the schooling of the young people concerned. There seems little reason to doubt that a crucial way of starting to understand such problems is to talk to those who are suffering from them. There is undeniably, so it seems to me, a useful piece of research to be carried out on such issues. So what, ethically, is the problem?

The fundamental question seems to be the following: Is it appropriate morally to encourage this particular young woman to undertake this particular piece of research? This is not a student with any professional skills of a therapeutic and counselling kind. There is nothing to suggest she has any special knowledge and understanding of the issues surrounding eating disorders such as anorexia and bulimia. She has no ready access to those services specializing in such distressing conditions to whom she might turn for help. This is already a particularly vulnerable group who may be further distressed in all kinds of unpredictable ways by talking (even if they have 'consented' to such discussions about their problems) to a young woman, no matter how sympathetic. The potential for distress and, maybe, real harm seems palpable. I leave out of the equation the annoyance and offence felt by (some) parents at the outcomes (again even if they have 'consented' to their children being interviewed). The one undeniable good that might come out of such a scenario is a well-written, perceptive piece on the plight of these young women, that suffices to meet the assignment requirements of the third year of the degree course being followed. The question that needs asking is whether the decision to proceed with the research should be more influenced by the possible harm done to vulnerable young girl students than by the formal satisfaction of a degree requirement. I suspect most of us would think that the potential harms outweigh the possible good of a decent research report and, of course, the serving of the interests of the undergraduate student concerned.

This is not to claim there should be a bar to research on the educational problems of vulnerable groups. It is to say, however, that where it is evident further harm may be done by a piece of research, every effort should be made to ensure that the research is conducted by those with the kind of skills that will minimize the risk of such harm. Furthermore, researchers should have access to services that can aid those who might be distressed by talking about issues germane to the research. One ought not to engage in research which carries a significant risk of upset and harm to those being researched. How significant the risk of distress and harm is can be importantly influenced by both the skills, maturity and experience of the researcher, and his or her ready access to the specialized skills that can help to alleviate the harm and distress brought about by the research experience. The moral point is plain: to engage in research which reasonably foreseeably will occasion harm and distress to research subjects is *prima facie* objectionable. The gratuitous infliction of harm upon another human raises the largest moral anxieties. Whether there are countervailing considerations that persuade us to proceed nevertheless with research, even if we suspect harm to the interests of the researched, presents some of the hardest problems confronting researchers striving to advance our knowledge and understanding. These concerns will emerge as we look at the other stages of research more generally.

The lesson of all the foregoing is simple enough: Getting clear about your research concerns is not simply finding a form of words representing the research to be undertaken. It also involves thinking through the conduct of the research, the problems and issues that foreseeably might arrive during the research process. If a topic is clearly sensitive, if it might be challenging to those being researched, if your interactions with the objects of your research might be fraught in ways causing upset, and so on, all reflect on whether the research proposed can justifiably be undertaken. There will clearly be circumstances in which it might be. But researchers do well to remember that their interest in the research is personal: for example, getting an MA, obtaining a doctorate, successfully completing an undergraduate assignment. The demands of morality go beyond the merely personal and embrace what it is right to do overall. There will be relatively few occasions in educational research where the sheer significance of what is being explored will justify overriding the significant interests of others. Truth (with a very big 'T') is very rarely indeed the outcome of, or indeed the ambition of, social scientific research. And what is true more generally, is strikingly evident in respect of educational research. Educational research is the target of much criticism. Foremost among the criticisms is the complaint that the product of so much research is trivial, barely worth knowing. What must be true is that the less significant truths can be invoked to set against the distress and harm that predictably is caused to those researched, the more it seems that moral considerations will act as a constraint upon researchers, to a greater degree more than they might like to acknowledge.

During the conduct of research, moral anxieties arising from the research process might assail the researcher in all kinds of unpredictable ways. They will demand a moral response. Where it is clear that issues which are candidates for research have the potential to be distressing or harmful to those being researched – because they are members of an, for example, already vulnerable group – the closest attention must be paid to the suitability of research being pursued. In those instances, particular attention needs to be paid to whether the researcher is the right person to undertake such research. Do they have the sensitivities, the professional skills that will avoid the distress and harm that an investigation inappropriately engaged in might generate?

It ought to be borne in mind at this stage that distress, harm, and feelings of having been taken advantage of arising from the chosen research topic need not arise only at the time of the enquiry. It might be a matter of realizing at the stage of the writing up of the research that there are grounds of moral complaint. For example, even if we allow (as surely we must) that outsiders can have authentic insights into another culture's practices, it might easily be that on a given occasion the inadequacy of the research done, its misrepresentations of another's cultural practices and customs, justifiably draws moral complaint. The topic chosen clearly had the potential to morally affront if not handled appropriately. This researcher from this kind of background, being the kind of person he or she was, with only a reasonable degree of foresight was not the person to do such sensitive research. We should be on the look-out for morally-sensitive research topics which, of their very nature, have the potential to create moral affront if not adequately handled. An educational researcher known to be a racist bigot looks to be unpromising material to do research into why it might be that Caribbean children are under-performing in a particular area of the curriculum compared to their white middle-class peers. The example is stark. The point is clear. Choosing a research issue demands a certain moral scrutiny. It is certainly no part of the research enterprise to cause harm gratuitously, to damage the interests of the researched. Except in the extremely unlikely event of a piece of educational/social research being of momentous significance, revelatory of some profound truth, we should avoid research that damages others. All research should be conducted with a view to serving the ends of knowing and understanding *consonant* with what is permitted morally. It is not a matter of intentionally pressing ahead with research while recognizing its morally problematic nature. Being negligent (which is the much more likely possibility) to such possibilities also attracts, quite properly, moral condemnation.

4

The Principle of Consent

One idea above all others dominates talk about the ethics of research involving (live) human beings: fully informed voluntary consent. Every code of ethics designed to guide research involving human subjects gives primacy to the requirement of fully informed voluntary consent on the part of the individuals concerned. The very clear presumption is that research involving human subjects undertaken without the explicit consent of the researched lacks an adequate moral basis, and it would be better if the research were not undertaken. Putting it the other way, if research is conducted on the basis of lack of consent, very compelling reasons indeed must be forthcoming to justify the research. The literature on the merits or otherwise of overt as against covert research is testimony to the claim that consent should underlie research involving human subjects. Of course, the fact that such a debate rumbles on also suggests a certain impatience on the part of some that the research effort should be so constrained by moral scruples. Overt research involves seeking and ensuring the consent at each stage of research of those involved in the research. The clearest instance of covert research would be researchers systematically concealing from the subjects of research at every stage that the research was being undertaken and that they were the objects of the research. There is no shortage in the literature of such deception being practiced. The justification, if any, will clearly lie in the value of the research undertaken, the value of the knowing and understanding now possessed as a consequence of the deception.

Before exploring such issues in more detail, let us understand more clearly why there is such an emphasis upon consent, what the required consent amounts to and how we might seek to guarantee we have consent. In addition, given consent is deemed desirable, we need to ask ourselves from whom consent should be forthcoming and how far consent runs.

The contemporary emphasis upon consent arises in important part from the outrages practiced in the name of science during the Second World War. Appalling indignities were inflicted upon Jews, gypsies, homosexuals and many, many others by Nazi doctors who, without consent, used them as guinea pigs in the pursuit of medical science. In the aftermath of the Second World War and the appreciation of the horrors inflicted upon huge numbers of people without their consent, there emerged a felt need to reaffirm in the clearest terms that any interference with the bodies, and in the lives, of other human beings should only be on the basis of their consent to such interference. The moral imperative that before invading the physical integrity of others in the name of medicine we should seek their consent to treatment or research has by extension and analogy informed the ethical codes governing the conduct of social scientific research. Sociologists, psychologists, educational researchers – all have codes of ethics which highlight the need to obtain the consent of research subjects. In the present climate, all funding agencies providing financial support for research will have as part of their protocol a requirement that informed consent on the part of the researched must be sought and forthcoming. Insistence upon consensually-grounded research is very much the order of the day. The expectation is that researchers seek the informed consent of those who are to be parties to research. It is bypassing informed consent that has to be justified. What considerations might justify research which is not grounded in informed consent is a matter of significant and contentious debate.

Whatever consent is, it involves more than merely assenting to or going along with suggestions made. This is captured in the insistence that consent be fully informed and voluntary. I go along with your suggestions when you hold a gun against my head and tell me what to do. Whatever coercion is, it is exemplified by doing something for fear of your life or of violence at the hands of another. My decision to do as you ask is only in the most Pickwickian sense *my* decision. What happens in such circumstances is clearly down to you rather than me. My will has simply been overridden. The insistence that consent be fully informed and voluntary demands of the researcher that he or she makes as clear as possible to those from whom consent is sought what is involved in the research. In the same way as a doctor seeking the informed consent of a patient should explain what the proposed treatment might involve – what the risks are of having the treatment as against not having it, how painful it will be, whether it is absolutely necessary, etc. – so our researcher should satisfy certain informational require-ments: what the research is about (its aims and purposes), what the research will involve, what will be expected of those whose consent is being sought, how much time and effort it will take on their part, how the data will be col-lected, whether they will be allowed to comment on the data collected and the interpretations placed upon the data, what the ultimate fate is of the research, whether it is to be published, and so on. A person has been fully informed if he has had explained to him anything that reasonably and foreseeably might influence the decision whether or not to agree to be a participant in the research. Deliberately not to reveal to individuals a consideration that is clearly germane to any likely decision on their part to agree to be part of the research effort (for fear they might be discouraged from giving their consent) is to diminish the significance of the 'consent' that might be forthcoming. Any decision made on the basis of ignorance connived at by the researcher who stands to benefit from the agreement to be a research subject is less than fully informed – and indeed, obviously involves deception.

To be voluntary, the decision arrived at to participate in research should be free of unwarranted pressures upon the individual arriving at that decision. The overriding of the capacity to decide for oneself can take an endless variety of forms. The ethics of research is insistent that consent given should be voluntary. At the very least, it discourages exploiting power (either one's own or that of a significant other in the life of the sought-for participant) to compel individuals to go along with one's research ambitions. Ideally, there should be no doubt that consent to the research enterprise on the part of a research subject should be *his* decision and no one else's. A headteacher signed up for an MA should not use her position to suggest to a member of her staff that she will mediate more enthusiastically on his behalf with the school governing body in the matter of the head of department job that is coming up very soon on the condition that he consent to being participant in her research. Using the language of coercion rather than inducements, she should not intimate that she will make it certain he does not get the job should he refuse. Voluntariness can be affected by both fear and inducements amounting to bribes. Many researchers will not, of course, be in a position to try to override the voluntary nature of consent. Power relations go both ways, and large numbers of researchers will be wholly dependent on others giving their consent on the basis of an adequate understanding of what the research involves. They will have given their consent because they are fully informed. Decisions arrived at in the light of a clear appreciation of all relevant factors are, absent with coercion, voluntary.

One could elaborate at great length on the notions of *fully informed* consent and *voluntary* consent but the point is surely clear enough. If consent is being sought, the researcher should do all he or she reasonably can to ensure the information made available, and the conditions under which it is received and (as it were) processed encourage the belief that consent granted is fully informed and voluntarily given. If a researcher is wholeheartedly driven by the ethical imperative of such consent, then if he or she has suspicions that the consent has been given very grudgingly because of pressure from above (to take our headteacher again, she wishes to be involved in a prestigious DfES funded research project and makes it very plain she would view with deep misfavour any teacher who refused to give time to the researcher), the researcher has to make a decision about whether to proceed with that element of the research in the light of the non-consensual nature of the agreement. We will look a little later at what might be involved in making such a decision.

If all relevant information (it will of course vary from instance to instance, from piece of research to piece of research) has been given, there is nothing to disturb the assumption consent has been given freely (as we say). In such circumstances it is reasonable to assume the requirement of consent has been met. The circumstances informing our discussion of consent so far have been of an uncomplicated kind. The context of seeking consent has been exemplary in this manner. It has largely been rooted in a model of one adult researcher addressing the informational needs of another adult so as to allow him or her to arrive at a considered judgement as to whether to help in the conduct of research. We have only hinted at the complications that undermine our simple model of consent as fully informed and voluntarily given. Our working presumption, in the circumstances outlined, that, other things being equal, consent has been given seems entirely reasonable. Given the extraordinary complexities surrounding the motivations of humans and their decision-making processes, if we are looking for so-called cast-iron guarantees that consent is fully informed and voluntary, probably none can be forthcoming. It would seem to be good practice to establish publicly the giving of consent by documenting it through a written statement by individuals to the effect they have consented and are fully aware of what they have consented to. Presuming consent on the part of the researched because they have not objected to the research going on seems out of keeping with the spirit of laying such emphasis upon the need for fully informed consent. Discussion of consent in political philosophy has played around with the notion of consent being given *tacitly*. There seems no place for such a notion in the realm of social scientific research. What simply cannot be countenanced as satisfying the consent requirement is undertaking research without the consent of those researched and then retrospectively telling them about the research, as if in so telling one has put the initial failure (refusal) to seek consent right. To have deliberately concealed from others that they were/have been the objects of research is to have engaged in deception. While not wishing to rule out of court the existence of reasons for concealing the truth of what was going on that might be justificatory of the deception – the sheer importance of the research, for instance – we need to insist upon a recognition that there can be no such thing as *retrospective* consent. As Wittgenstein might say, 'That is a conceptual point'.

Nothing has been said so far about why the seeking of consent is seen as such a fundamental (ethical) requirement of the research process. To pursue this very far is to take us into some of the most fundamental issues in moral philosophy. Invoking the importance of consent on the part of those affected by our actions brings in its wake the invoking of such key morally-significant notions as autonomy, self-determination, privacy, the right to privacy, respect for persons, treating individuals as ends in themselves rather than as means, trust as an integral feature of human intercourse, and so on. Thus, consent should always be sought as a tribute to the autonomy of individuals. Additionally, it should be sought because there are some things (thoughts, feelings, attitudes, etc.) that are private to the individuals concerned, and it is only their consent that can justify entering into that domain of essentially private concerns. Also, if we ride roughshod over the wishes of others, we do damage to the fabric of trust that sustains human relationships. We could go on. In our society there is a strong intuition about the ultimate importance attached to individuals owning their lives which they may or may not, in specified circumstances, be prepared to share with others.

Talk of consent also points us in the direction of competing moral theories that explain why consent is such a salient feature of much human interaction. For instance, utilitarians who look to the consequences of actions as determining the rightness (or not) of actions will emphasize how seeking consent and acting accordingly will encourage trust between individuals. Once trust is assailed, the suspicion of the research community in the eyes of the wider public (say) will be to the detriment of the research effort. Kantians will insist that avoiding consent is a way of *using* people that is not in keeping with the dignity and respect that as persons they should be accorded and, as such, not to be tolerated. Justifications of the importance attached to consent will draw upon different moral traditions and (as already briefly mentioned), while drawing upon a familiar vocabulary will offer us different accounts of how consent stands justified in terms of that vocabulary. Be all that as it may, there surely can be no doubt that if as a moral community we ceased to cling onto the fundamental importance of consent in human affairs, we would have lost that sense of the importance of individuals to which as a society we attach such significance. It really is very unclear why the research community should be excused the powerful presumption that, wherever possible, consent should be sought.

The hard questions that consent throws up (ethically) for the researcher are clearly not exhausted by the simple model of consent with which we have been working. Once the emphasis is upon consent as fully informed and voluntary, it is clear other questions clamour for our attention. What about those who, either as proper objects of research concern or sources of data (children, the mentally disabled, the mentally disturbed), cannot (or are certainly so deemed) give consent that is informed and voluntary? On what basis can we proceed to carry out research involving them? When consent is given prior to the research being undertaken, how far does that consent run? What reasonably can we infer must have been consented to? How do we distinguish between those facets of research activity which we can be confident are covered by the consent given and those which – if only because (even) we ourselves did not quite envisage the research going in quite the direction it is now going, for example – we can be fairly certain were never within the minds of those who initially consented that issues now being pursued would be pursued? And does all of this suggest we should, if serious about the ethical imperative of consent, embrace a more 'process driven' model of consent: one in which we seek continually to renew our mandate, as it were, for the conduct of our research with those who are lending themselves to our research endeavour?

How can we find an accommodation between such questions and their answers, and the independent claims the research enterprise makes upon us? What I mean by this last question is that we must expect times when tensions arise between ethical claims upon us that we normally recognize as demanding satisfaction, and our own investments of energy, time and ambition in the research. It is easy to conceive of situations in which, with consent given to a particular research agenda and set of concerns, as the research unfolds other issues emerge which seem to the researcher to be much more interesting (perhaps, even much more important). If only one concealed the altered direction of the research, really interesting and challenging outcomes of the research could be on the cards. The fear might be that to seek a renewal of consent to pursue these other questions will lead to the withdrawal of consent, and with it goes a huge investment of time and energy already given to the research – as well as the possibility of that doctorate.

Consider the following scenario: A doctoral candidate gets consent from a headteacher to investigate the delivery of a programme of multicultural education in a given year group. She is particularly interested (and at the time she gets consent, genuinely so) in the dynamics between the cultural groups making up the year group. Sensitive to the ethical imperative, she has also sought the explicit consent of the teachers in whose classes she will be conducting her research. This is not a researcher who thinks that the consent of the headteacher counts as consent on the part of all those others who will aid her in her research project. Let us suppose this researcher has also sought the consent of the parents of the year group and the very children who are the occasion of her research. In all instances, she was inspired by the doctrine of full informed consent. One of her clear beliefs is that whatever the situation in medicine, where the sheer complexity of the issues involved might make it difficult to believe that educated fully informed consent on the part of most patients can truly be forthcoming, there is little reason to suppose that in social scientific research in general (and educational research in particular), at least among adults, something more resembling fully informed consent cannot (and should not) be established – although she does in part think that seeking the consent of young children (how young being a matter for some debate) to the research process is more of a gesture than anything else.

So far, so good. What happens if once the research is under way, the researcher suddenly realizes the most interesting and most important factors bearing upon the delivery of multicultural education in the year group lie removed from the children and their relationships. It is the teachers, their competences, attitudes and outlooks, that become key, and to the researcher really problematic. She very much suspects (or even just fears) that to reveal her new focus of attention will lead to a withdrawal of consent on the part of the school, and in particular the teachers. She could remain quiet, and collect relevant data in line with her new research agenda while ostensibly conducting her research as originally envisaged. In effect, what was an overt research exercise would become an exercise in covert research. She is now really perplexed. How hard should she cling to her belief in fully informed consent, is she able to persuade herself that an ethical case can be made out to justify proceeding with her research in these very changed circumstances?

The distinction between overt and covert research is

plain enough in principle. If wholly committed to a process-driven model of consent, a researcher will always be engaged in overt research. The process model involves collaboration with other participants in the research at all stages of the research – in embracing the research questions, keeping everyone informed as to what is happening as the research unfolds, alerting individuals to (and seeking their agreement in) the changed emphases of the research, getting interviewees to check over transcripts, showing them the analysis of their data, sharing conclusions with them, and so on.

Of course, for reasons of self-interest, or for reasons more intrinsic to the research itself, the process model can be followed with greater or less enthusiasm. Resort to deception in the sense of not being fully upfront about aspects of the research is always possible, and for exactly the same reasons as previously intimated. There cannot be any doubt that too high-minded an approach to issues of consent – premised on either a process or event model of consent – can get in the way of the research imperative, driven as it is by the desire to understand something that the researcher thinks demands a better understanding. While it is rarely, if ever, the case that research into social phenomena *transforms* our comprehension of such phenomena, there are many socially problematic issues which, for all kinds of very respectable reasons, we rightly think it would be to all of our benefits to be able to explain and understand very much more than we do. An overwhelming impetus to social scientific research is the sense that we owe it to ourselves to subject our social practices and behaviours to critical scrutiny. We take seriously the maxim about the 'unexamined life is not worth living' and apply it more generally to human phenomena. But also, it is rational to believe that the better informed we are about our practices and conduct, the more likely it is we can formulate policies grounded in evidence so as to make our affairs go better – both ethically, and with a view to achieving the ends we set ourselves.

In respect of our researcher, we can throw into the equation the significant personal investment in the research and its possibilities. Acting ethically does not demand of an agent a complete self-denial of his or her own interests. We may have here a researcher who has given large amounts of time to the conduct of research, who is seeking a doctorate to further a career which in turn will provide an income that will sustain the lives of those who depend in part upon the researcher – aged parents or young children, for example.

No extant ethical code of practice designed to govern the actions of researchers is so draconian as to suggest that consent must always be forthcoming at all times, either initially or at every stage during the research. There is always a 'let out' clause recognizing that, in some circumstances, consent may not be necessary or that the researcher might be justified in not seeking it. Less helpfully, little guidance is given about what these circumstances are. Since ethical codes of practice characteristically lay down *principles* to guide behaviour, it is not surprising little substantive guidance is forthcoming in respect of actual instances demanding a moral response to those circumstances by the researcher. Principles are unqualified, highly abstract assertions giving expression to values designed to govern our conduct. 'Always treats persons as ends in themselves rather than as means to an end' is a principle. 'The researcher has an overriding obligation to truth' is a principle often laid down to shape the actions of the researcher. The very abstract nature of principles demands interpretation as to just what they demand in given circumstances. The fact that principles can pull in different ways when confronted by a particular state of affairs poses further acute problems for the agent looking to them for guidance. The particularities of the situations in which researchers find themselves and the moral quandaries thrown up by a given set of facts rule out the possibility of a simple application of competing principles to the circumstances of the case. Adjudication between competing principles is never a straightforward matter. It goes to the very heart of how we resolve moral perplexities. None of this, however, is to cast doubt upon the value of codes of practice which remind researchers that research not proceeding on the basis of consent stands in need of justification. Presumptively, consent should be sought: 'Always seek consent' may stand as a principle in its own right, or as an interpretive reading of the maxim 'Always treats persons as ends in themselves rather than as means to an end.' Whatever, there will always be situations where the demand for consent stands uneasily alongside the commitment to the pursuit of truth.

5

On Confidentiality

Before saying more about what is involved in confronting the moral issues any kind of research might generate, and about how a researcher might start to resolve to his or her own satisfaction those concerns, let me say a little about another principle closely associated with the principle of consent: the principle of confidentiality. The first point to make is that they are not the same. Consent will often not be forthcoming unless confidentiality can be guaranteed. But it is clearly conceivable that someone might consent to the research, irrespective of whether their confidentiality is guaranteed or not. Investigative journalism, surely a species of research on matters of very great social importance, is full of examples of evidence given consensually, where the source of information is perfectly happy to lend their name publicly to the exercise. Contrariwise, even if guaranteed confidentiality and knowing that the guarantee is watertight, someone will refuse consent. *As a matter of fact*, the evidence suggests that, as part of the negotiations for consent, assurances of confidentiality will go a long way to securing consent. Confidentiality is best assured on the basis of anonymizing the collection of data. The research methods literature is full of advice as to how to achieve such anonymity for participants in research. A researcher undertaking to ensure the confidentiality of their informants subsequently stands under an obligation to discharge that obligation. Whatever the precise relationships between the principles of consent and confidentiality, there can be no doubt that in the vast majority of instances failure to guarantee confidentiality will sabotage attempts to obtain consent.

There exists a significant literature given over to establishing the ethical grounding of confidentiality in research involving human participants. There is a literature that highlights the benefits to the conduct of research if the researched feel confident in the guarantees of confidentiality offered. Another tradition sees the principle of confidentiality as an appropriate response to the importance of privacy in human affairs. Participants in research will not reveal their real feelings, opinions, or attitudes about the job, the institutions, their colleagues, the policies they are having to institute, and so on unless confidentiality is assured. The analogy with medicine is plain: unless the patient–doctor relationship is confidential, the relationship will be seriously impaired. The revealing of symptoms is much aided if the patient can be assured that those symptoms will not become public knowledge. More fully informed, the doctor can better do his job of prescribing appropriate treatment. The asking of help from professionals privy to issues from which patients are seeking relief (physical or mental) would be diminished, absent the guaranteeing of confidentiality. The researcher seeking an accurate understanding of some social practice or phenomena needs data fit for the purpose. Anything that encourages openness and frankness in the giving of data can only serve the good of the research.

Perhaps more influential in the contemporary climate as justificatory of the importance of confidentiality is the proclaimed right to privacy. The principle of confidentiality is tribute to the importance we attach to the right to privacy; or if not the *right* to privacy, the importance of privacy in human affairs. Talk of privacy, and the right to privacy, gestures in the direction of what we (rightly) glimpse to be an integral element of our belief that individuals matter. It is difficult to believe that anything would be left of the notion, so fundamental to the structure of our moral thinking, that persons are deserving of respect and have inherent dignity unless there was recognition of the significance of privacy in our affairs.

While on the one hand this is to say everything, it is on the other to say almost nothing; What is privacy? What function does it serve in our lives? Just why is it so important? Are there distinctive spheres of concern in respect of which privacy is most justifiably to be invoked? How can we adjudicate between its claims and the claims of the rest of to have access to certain information? One could go on. In short, we surely know privacy is important. But we struggle (and this is a typical philosophical perplexity) if asked to state unambiguously *why* it is so important. We are certain there are things about ourselves and our affairs, our opinions about others, our feelings and attitudes, our personal habits and practices, we would prefer others did not know and which we would feel they have no right to know. We would feel bruised, violated, harmed, if others had found out and made public what we would prefer to keep private. And we would be justified in our sense of outrage. However, in respect of 'private' matters, it is always open to us to agree to share those concerns with others, if so minded. And it is further open to us to agree to share in a manner of our choosing. We can strike a contract with those with we share, demanding of them that confidentiality is preserved. Confidentiality is the price demanded for the sharing, and ensuring confidentiality the 'consideration' (as the lawyers would put it) the researcher gives for being privy to the innermost thoughts and feelings of the participant in her research.

Once the guarantee of confidentiality is given, the researcher stands under a stringent (moral) obligation to do whatever is required to make certain confidentiality prevails. To be careless of the obligation is to do a moral harm to the source of privileged information. And it is certainly to do damage to the trust that needs to be in place between researchers and the researched if social scientific research is to flourish. Researchers have obligations to their fellow researchers. One of those obligations is not to conduct themselves in ways detrimental to the enterprise of research itself. If it is indeed the case that being careless of the confidentiality requirement violates the proper weight to be given to the role of privacy in our affairs, and if the effect is to be so damaging to the fabric of trust upon which the conduct of research so much depends, the claim of confidentiality upon the researcher is very demanding.

There exist clear expectations that researchers will seek the consent of the participants in research, and guarantee confidentiality for those who advance the research agenda of the researcher by being sources of information. In both instances, it is the violation of the requirement of confidentiality and consent that demands justification. We might say there is a *prima facie* obligation upon researchers to seek and be satisfied that consent has been given, and that where guarantees of confidentiality have been proffered and taken up, sought and agreed to, in like manner the researcher stands under a *prima facie* obligation in respect of the principle of confidentiality. Questions which have always haunted researchers have been whether consent should always be sought, or whether there are occasions in which the principle of confidentiality can be overridden. There has always been a robust body of opinion within the social scientific community which has chafed at the restrictions imposed upon the researcher by the imperative of consent. Less contentiously, there have always been instances in which researchers worry that clinging on to the principle of confidentiality might make the researcher complicit in some greater moral wrong. Let's explore the issue of confidentiality first.

Taking confidentiality seriously does not only mean intentionally taking it upon oneself not to reveal to others what has been revealed in confidence. It also places a burden upon the researcher to make sure confidentiality is not breached by accident or as a consequence of carelessness in the handling of data. The researcher needs to be sensitive to how things might go wrong. The test in this connection must surely be whether he or she has taken into account everything that reasonably and foreseeably could be taken into account. What counts as 'reasonably foreseeable' is a moving feast. Once alerted to other ways in which confidentiality runs the risk of being infringed, those ways must then be taken on board. A colleague of mine was recently examining a doctoral thesis. The candidate had gone to great lengths, via anonymizing all the data, to ensure the confidentiality of the respondents. To help set the scene, she briefly out-lined the context of the research, and to this end, she quoted half an anodyne sentence from a recent OFSTED report upon the school which was the focal point of her research. Almost for something to do, my colleague fed this fragment of a sentence into the search engine and was startled to have before him the relevant OFSTED report, thus identifying the school. A couple more clicks on the computer and he was in possession of data allow-ing him to identify, if so minded, all the respondents who had contributed data to the doctoral submission. What technologically really would have been unimaginable even two years earlier had now allowed a tearing-down of the veil of confidentiality.

Of course, it is inconceivable that guarantees in the

matter of confidentiality will never be found wanting. But there are too many instances in the literature indicating cases in which for want of just a little more care, distress and sometimes real hardship to sources of evidence could and should have been avoided. If the researcher has pledged him or herself to preserve confidentiality, it is morally incumbent upon them to strive to conduct the research in ways which, as far as humanly possible, avoid disclosure that might embarrass those who have given their time and energy to further the research effort.

More plainly a case of moral anxiety is the situation where in the course of research things are said or information is conveyed which puts the researcher in the invidious situation of knowing things which are of moral significance and which touch the vital interests of others. A particularly striking example from psychotherapy dramatically exemplifying such possibilities is the famous case of *Tarasoff*. Briefly, a psychotherapist was informed in the course of therapy that the patient intended to kill another person. This he subsequently did. The family sued on the grounds that they had not been informed of the threat to their daughter. The therapist claimed he was bound by the principle of confidentiality and by a proper respect for the patient's right to privacy. The court ruled (but not unanimously) that the public interest in safety from violent assault outweighed the patient's right to his privacy. In short, the principle of confidentiality in specified circumstances can be outweighed by more compelling moral considerations.

Issues of confidentiality, of course, take on a particularly striking hue in the medical sciences where matters (literally) of life and death are at stake. Consider a doctor pondering on whether to alert a spouse to the fact her husband is HIV positive, when the husband had gone to the doctor to establish whether he was HIV and insisted upon patient confidentiality in the matter despite his evident intent not to tell his wife about his condition. These are matters of agonizing moral significance about which rational and well-intentioned individuals can disagree profoundly. In the case of *Tarassof* the dissenting judgement is a powerful restatement of the fundamental importance of confidentiality in the therapeutic relationship, so fundamental indeed that in the opinion of the judge the duty to preserve confidentiality rightly outweighed any duty to warn about the *possible* murder of the girl. There is no reason to suppose that moral conflicts involving confidentiality are to be disposed of easily.

So what of the principle of confidentiality in the sphere of social and educational research? It is difficult to accept that the commitment to confidentiality can or should be absolutely unqualified. Such a commitment would entail that no matter what the researcher might find out about, and from, individuals to whom the pledge of confidentiality has been given, under no circumstances should he or she divulge anything that he or she is now privy to arising from the conduct of the research. While recognizing that considerations of trust are important, that the fact of having made a promise is morally significant, and that disregarding the imperative of confidentiality has the capacity to damage the research community, we surely also recognize that more morally compelling than all of these factors is the obligation to do what we can to avert great harms that might befall others. If this requires the breaching of guarantees of confidentiality given, so be it. Morally, we can do no other.

While at the level of principle it is easy to appeal to such a shared moral sentiment, we must not suppose that in practice it will be easy to decide what to do in the particular instance. What to do if, in the course of school-based research into some aspect of teacher–pupil relationships, the researcher becomes uneasy about the (unduly sexualized, as it appears to the researcher) conduct of a teacher towards his or her young charges? What if it seems plain to the researcher that a teacher operating within a ethnically-diverse school is clearly racist in attitudes demonstrated towards some of the children? What if all the evidence given to a researcher by the pupils in a class or school makes it plain that a given teacher is hopelessly bad at the job and is harming all of their prospects but that the school, for its own reasons, is turning a blind eye to such incompetence? What if a teacher openly confesses to sexual misconduct with pupils over the years? And so on and so on. Confidentiality can bring with it burdens arising from the very information the commitment to the preservation of confidentiality facilitates. It is a matter of judgement whether the moral conflicts arising from a commitment to confidentiality are as stark and dramatic (or as frequent) in the social sciences as they are in the professions – the law, the various branches of medical practice (after all, what could be of more moral weight than issues of life and death, the enjoyment of freedom or not?). But conflicts certainly arise, and they create moral perplexities that have to be confronted. How they are to be resolved will be examined as part of the general discussion of how moral issues in social and educational research might be approached.

As already discussed, all ethical codes of practice designed to guide research involving humans lay a pre-eminent emphasis upon the importance of seeking and securing the consent of those involved in the research. Seeking consent can frequently, of course, not be evidence of a moral commitment to the importance of informed voluntary consent. Rather, it will be a recognition of certain brute realities confronting the researcher. The *pragmatics* of the situation demand you obtain consent to create even the possibility of the research getting off the ground. A young undergraduate doing an empirical study to satisfy his degree requirements and wishing to research the ethos of a school (say) must obtain the consent of the appropriate person in a school or schools to even be in a position to undertake his proposed research. Without such permission, the research is a non-starter. And many, many researchers wishing to explore aspects of institutions are dependent upon being granted entry by those who have it within their power to scupper research possibilities by simply denying would-be researchers permission to enter their school, factory, jail, or whatever it might be. Social research is dependent in large measure on the tolerance extended to researchers by those who 'gate-keep' institutions. Ethical guidelines laid down by the various professional bodies emphasize the moral significance of consent by tying in the seeking of consent with moral imperatives such as recognition of human dignity, or seeing other individuals as ends in themselves rather than using them as means to ends. Putting it shortly, seeking informed voluntary consent is to show respect for persons. There is, of course, no tension between having to gain consent and the advice offered in ethical guidelines for human research that the consent should be informed and voluntary. The need to get consent so as to get into an institution for research purposes should not involve deception. It is still incumbent upon those seeking consent to provide all that is required to allow for informed and voluntary consent by those whose permission is so desperately needed.

6

Further Issues about Consent

As briefly mentioned previously, there have always been voices impatient with the constraints imposed upon the conduct of research by the need for ethical dealings with participants in research. Putting it another way, there have always been those who devotion to the cause of truth and research has caused them to think that a bit of deception here and there may be no bad thing, or in extreme cases that wholesale deception can be justified in the name of truth and the significance of the research undertaken. One might think of it as an undiluted version in the human sciences of the pursuit of knowledge for its own sake as a self-justifying activity.

At the level of the actual conduct of research, it has frequently taken the form of suggesting that the knowledge of the participants in the research that research is going on falsifies the very data the research was designed to better understand. Intuitively this seems an appealing idea. If a researcher has explained carefully to consenting male teachers that the research is being undertaken to explore how gender stereotyping enters into the dealings of male teachers with those they teach, it seems at least plausible to imagine that the behaviour of the male teachers being researched might be significantly and self-consciously different to how they might typically conduct themselves in the classroom. Research that aspires to be as naturalistic as it can possibly be might sit uneasily with too much awareness on the part of those in the native setting as to what is going on. The point is clear enough. The researched will say things or act in ways differently from how they would normally, just because they know what is going on. From the research perspective, knowledge can be a dangerous thing.

The issue of consent can be rendered problematic at two levels: arguments are advanced that suggest 1) that the *prima facie* claim of consent as a prerequisite for the conduct of research is not compelling, and 2) that even if it is, in the particular circumstances of a given researcher a case can be made for why the normal requirement of consent can be set aside. Disputing the *prima facie* requirement of consent is to suggest that the obsession, with consent which lies at the heart of all ethical codes of practice is simply that: an obsession, which does damage to the research agenda. Whether we seek consent or not will simply be a matter of tactic, not a requirement of morality. The weaker case that claims the presupposition of consent can in specified circumstances be set aside amounts to saying that the commitment to consent can be outweighed by other sets of considerations. What those considerations might be will be dependent on the circumstances of the case, and will vary from situation to situation.

The radical assault on the moral requirement of consent in the matter of human research involves a cluster of considerations, such as: the benefits that will flow from the unconstrained pursuit of social research; the pursuit of knowledge as self-justifying, and the paramount importance of the principle of scientific freedom in our affairs. Any one of these considerations demands sustained and independent treatment. Let's briefly deal with each in turn.

Part of the dream of many researchers of human phe-

nomena is that with the greater insight and understanding research will afford us, we will be able to make
things simply go better than they otherwise do. Institutions will serve their purposes better, and activities and
practices exposed to the light of day through research will
be better seen for what they are – as deeply irrational or
highly dangerous – and therefore abandoned. If we better
understood the culture of hospitals, jails, schools and
universities, and care homes for young children, if we had
better insight into the sources of religious and ethnic
tensions (the list can be indefinitely multiplied), possessed of knowledge we could more effectively deliver
socially-desirable ends. The heyday of the optimism that
once drove the social scientific community as it strove to
emulate the extraordinary explanatory power of the
advanced physical sciences (and all the technology such
power produced in its wake) is long gone. While never
wanting to doubt that social research has uncovered for
us all kinds of interesting and immensely worthwhile
insights, there is a much greater acceptance of the fact
that most outcomes of research into human practices,
institutions and activities are at best interesting, and
rarely, if ever, transforming. It is not even obvious that
putting together all we have found out in an area of
sustained research interest (so called evidence–based
research) can give us much in the way of stunning
insights to which the rest of us are indebted. The lament,
once very commonly heard, that the social sciences
merely confirm to us what we already know, while always
too crude an assessment of the outcomes of research, did
capture something of the inconclusive nature of much of
it. Deceiving the researched – either by lying or by some
other method – represents an intrusion into lives, private
or public, that demands justification. So deeply entren-
ched a feature of our moral universe as the belief that
individuals have a moral standing and dignity that places

in us a duty to respect them is not so easily to be set aside on the altar of the alleged (and, as yet, barely forthcoming) benefits flowing from social research. Possible benefits cannot outweigh the moral imperative of seeking the consent of those whose lives researchers intrude upon.

The proposition that the pursuit of knowledge is self-justifying is frequently heard. There are general problems surrounding the significance and validity of this claim. In this particular context, it simply amounts to the claim that no moral considerations should constrain the seeking of knowledge. The acquisition of knowledge stands above and apart from normal moral constraints. Truth (with a very big T indeed) becomes our overriding goal.

No doubt, there are many things we might come to know if we proceeded irrespective of the morality of what we are doing. No doubt, there are many things we might lend ourselves to in the pursuit of knowledge, oblivious to the demands of morality. We already have the awful example of the Nazis as testimony to the practice of research untouched by the dictates of morality. The proposition that we should disregard the rights of research subjects over their own lives in the name of knowledge and understanding has only to be stated to offend our deepest moral convictions. This is not to deny the importance of 'truth' as a goal of human endeavour. It is to remind us that this is attainable on the basis of individuals giving their consent to being participants in research. It is to emphasize the problematic nature of putting to one side the real moral harms we do to others if we ignore the requirement of consent in the name of those great abstractions; truth, knowledge, and understanding. Human research is research involving other fellow human beings. We diminish ourselves if we fail to recognize the moral burdens that lie upon us in our dealings with our fellow creatures. A sensitivity to the respect that should be accorded them, to their privacy, to the ownership of their own lives, should always be to the forefront of our minds. It seems entirely appropriate to ask a researcher who seeks to persuade us that the commitment to the principle of consent is morally gratuitous whether he would be quite so unconcerned if others lied to him, pried into his life, represented themselves as other than they were in the name of *their* research. If he would not, wherein lays the difference?

The physical world does not reveal its secrets and underlying mechanisms easily. It is a tribute to the human mind that we have been so successful in laying bare those secrets and explanatory mechanisms. We understand so much more, can accomplish so much more as a consequence of the triumph of the activities of physical scientists.

Such knowledge and understanding has spawned the outstanding technological and other achievements that have such significance in our lives. To a limited degree, we have lifted the veil on nature and its mysteries. A similar ambition has fuelled the activities of many in the social sciences. There are good reasons, however, to be sceptical about whether the social sciences can ever emulate the physical sciences in their scope and explanatory power. But this might simply be to say that different objects of understanding reward us with different kinds of understanding. It is how things are.

Nature does not set out to deceive us. It poses problems of understanding we may or may not be clever enough to overcome. Social and educational researchers also too have devised a variety of techniques to put them in a position to uncover and make sense of what is happening in human contexts. Which strategy or mix of strategies is best suited to understanding what is going on within a given social or educational context is an important concern for any researcher (other books in this series address these crucial matters). Fairly obviously, however, the strategies embraced will importantly relate to the context to be explored and the research questions to which answers are being sought. What has driven a certain disregard for issues of consent as a *prima facie* obligation to be met is a crucial disanalogy between the plight of the physical scientist and that of the social and educational researcher. Nature, while it poses problems, does not dissemble or seek intentionally to conceal or discourage research. The same can certainly not be said of humans in respect of their practices and concerns. Deceit, warning people off, censorship, denying access to information, misleading in a myriad of ways are all devices used to muddy the waters of our understanding of what is happening and going on.

It is easy to see how threatening such familiar features of our lives are to the idea of disinterested enquiry which has as its goal deeper knowledge and understanding of features of social life. It is equally easy to see how the recognition of such goings-on might encourage a certain impatience with the constraint of consent as a precondition of the conduct of social and educational research. It is not clear, however, that such considerations justify the disregarding of the presumption that consent should be sought. There may be specifiable circumstances in which a compelling case can be made out that bypassing consent is justified. We do well to recognize that there are available to the researcher all manner of means in which participants in research can be morally abused – hidden tape recorders, videos, secret filming. What is intolerable is the notion that researchers in pursuit of a degree, an MA, a doctorate, or even a large-scale piece of funded research can proceed with their interventions into others' lives and practices without due regard to those moral niceties which give expression to our sense of others' worth. To spy upon others, to deceive systematically in the conduct of our research, to intrude upon the lives of others without their consent is, except in the most extreme instances, to do a moral wrong. The working rule should be: consent should be sought. The emphasis upon consent is not only a moral imperative reflecting a proper regard for the participants in research, but also a recognition of the obligations owed to the wider research community. There can be no doubt that anything done which violates the trust between the research community and those whom researchers wish to better understand, and upon whom they are reliant for the very possibilities of research, is to the detriment of the wider research community. The individual researcher has responsibilities to the truth, to those being researched, and to the enterprise of human research itself.

Thus far, we have explored at a general level considerations pointing to the need to recognize the stringency of the obligation to seek consent. Arguments designed to make our attachment to the principle of consent provisional rather than *prima facie* have not carried conviction. Just to reiterate: an overriding principle driving research should be the getting of consent – fully informed and voluntary. This amounts not simply to the idea that we get consent if we find it necessary to do so, or that getting, consent will ease the way. It represents a settled conviction that consent must be sought, *unless* there is some overwhelming set of reasons that justify the setting aside of the requirement of consent. The issues of when and how we recognize and deal with the moral perplexities that will confront researchers as they go about their business is now our concern. Whether it is an issue arising from considerations of consent or an issue emerging from the research as it unfolds, the challenges to the researcher are very similar.

At this late stage, the discussion must be programmatic rather than as is detailed as is ideally required. How to confront and resolve moral problems is as fundamental an issue as there is in moral philosophy. If in the conduct of research the researcher is morally uncertain as to what she ought to do, how is she to proceed? What would constitute a satisfactory response to moral concern? Once an issue is identified as having ethical dimensions, a response is demanded. What should that response be?

We perhaps need to be a little careful here. In my experience (as mentioned earlier), the vast bulk of research done, certainly in the life of the tiro researcher, does not generate too much in the way of moral anxiety. And when it does, the 'ethical' issues thrown up are a mile away from the urgent moral problems that might confront a doctor or lawyer in their dealings with their clients. That is as it should be, and is only to be expected. Matters of life and death, guilt or innocence, are not the stuff of educational researchers, nor most social researchers. But moral problems there can undeniably be.

7

Moral Issues in Research

All researchers bring to the conduct of their research a mix of moral bits and pieces. What I mean by 'bits and pieces' is that what might be called our individual moral outlook is made up of some principles, attitudes, intuitions, stances upon particular issues, a more or less well-developed moral sense, character traits of appropriate kinds, and even (though often more implicit than explicit) what philosophers have called a meta-ethic. To elaborate just a little: principles are general rules we invoke to justify the more particular decisions we make. You ought not to have done X (some morally disapproved-of action) because X is wrong because (for example) you ought to treat all human beings with the same respect. The principle here called upon is an attachment to a principle of non-discrimination. Principles invoked to justify moral stances may or may not cohere well with each other within an individual life. I suspect relatively few of us have a consistent and highly-structured pattern of underlying principles that shape our moral responses. Rather, our moral outlook is a function of accretion over time, not of deep reflection going in the direction of consistency and coherency. As our lives have unfolded, as we have been subject to different experiences and to the opinions of others, so our moral outlook has been shaped.

This is not to say anything about whether greater

coherency in moral outlooks is a good or bad thing. It is simply to recognize the fragmented nature of our individual moral psyches. I might feel strongly about animal rights, the issues of abortion and euthanasia, the waging of war, the need for people to take responsibility for their own lives, and so on. An onlooker might be surprised at how I could consistently hold the constellation of particular views I do on such matters. Irrespective of alleged inconsistencies within those views, there is no doubt that they are for me matters of great moral import. I care about such issues in the right way for them to qualify unambiguously as matters of moral concern. I am stricken by remorse, feel guilt, if I behave in ways at variance with what I claim ought to be done or said. I seem to have a certain agonized moral integrity, while you seem rather casual about moral matters. I see moral concerns where you see none. I may well view it as a moral failing on your part that your moral sense is so much less well-developed than mine, while you may see my moral sensitivity as a form of moral pathology. I am horribly honest, determinedly courageous, driven by the need to cling to principles of moral action. You are honest but altogether more sensitive than I am to the likely impact of brutal honesty upon those around us. You are courageous enough, but not to the point of foolhardiness as you might think I am. Principled action has its place but not, you feel, if it means a blindness to the particularities of the different situations we are confronted with as moral agents. And finally, as befits my general high-mindedness, let us suppose my meta-ethic is one grounded in a fierce attachment to the place of individual rights in the moral universe. You, on the other hand, have a more utilitarian cast of mind and think that a concern for the consequences of actions – their impact upon human happiness and misery – is key to the moral evaluation of proposed actions. The ultimate difference between you and I as researchers might reveal itself in the fact that where I see a moral quandary, you see nothing to excite moral concern.

These sketches are no doubt inadequate in all kinds of ways. A much more sensitive taxonomy of the moral make-up of individuals is demanded, a more elaborated portrayal of the real differences between individuals as moral agents. But I hope the point is clear enough. We come to and confront moral issues as individuals who have to make up their own minds about how to act

Moral concerns can arise at all stages in the research process. As mentioned, there can be occasions when, despite the presumptive commitment to seeking consent, the research imperative might suggest deception in one of its guises would be the better way forward. Things might come to the attention of the researcher that prompt reflection whether the obligation to preserve confidentiality should be set aside. In the course of research, information, arising directly from the research or almost incidentally, comes to the attention of the researcher that he might well think he ought to make available to significant others. And, though much less of a problem for someone learning the craft (in my language, a tiro), the end product of the research – a document reporting upon the findings of the research – can raise important problems about the uses to which the research might be put, and who should have access to it

It is not uncommon nowadays – reflecting the importance attached to ethically-informed social and educational research – to set up ethics boards or committees to aid and give advice on ethical matters touching research. Certainly those applying to foundations for money to conduct research find, as a matter of course, they have to persuade the funding body of the ethical integrity of the proposed research. If they intend to practice some form of covert research, they will have to persuade the funding agency that they are justified in bypassing consent. Given the insistence in the relevant ethical codes upon the importance of having informed consent, the case will need to be compelling: but in some circumstances, permission may be forthcoming. The research is allowed to proceed (and be funded) on the basis of concealment of the true purposes of the research. Moral deliberation has occurred, resulting in permission to so proceed. What is true at the institutional level is now common at the level of the individual university student. Mechanisms are often put in place so that if a student has a moral anxiety, advice and guidance can be sought from a group of academics on the moral way forward. What are we to make of this determination of morality by committee?

We need to distinguish between seeking advice on moral matters, and hoping there is someone or a body to whom we can turn who can decide for us what ought to be done. Morality is as much a rational enterprise as any other. Whatever the final status of moral judgements, there is no reason to suppose that in the moral sphere anything goes. It is always appropriate to ask individuals to justify their moral choices and actions. The clear expectation is that reasons should be forthcoming for choices made and actions undertaken in the name of morality. Moral perplexities are susceptible to intellectual analysis. Many of the things we most agonize about are issues of moral moment: the waging of war, abortion, euthanasia, sexual relations, the freedom of the press, the right to live our lives as we see fit, obligations to future generations, the rights of children and so on. There is a litany of moral concerns that engage our intellectual energies. Raising concerns and sharing thoughts on such issues with others is not only common but a great aid to thinking more clearly about what is being disputed. Being sensitive to a moral dimension of your research and its possibilities may well encourage the thought that discussions with others might give you a richer appreciation of issues that should be taken into account.

Issues come in all shapes and sizes, and quite unexpectedly. To take sundry instances that have recently come to my attention: a doctoral candidate who was suddenly seized by the thought there was a moral issue about accessing emails sent to a key participant in her research. The emails and their content were highly relevant to her research concerns. The senders, however, did not have any idea that emails sent as private correspondence might be used as materials for research. The research project would be significantly enhanced by utilizing the materials of the emails. Should she seek permission from the senders? Was it enough that the recipient of the emails gave his permission to use the content of private correspondence? Was the fact her doctorate would be more significant if informed by these materials enough reason to ignore considerations of consent? Or again, a student who was anxious about the sheer incompetence of a teacher being seen during the conduct of research. It was her opinion that the teacher concerned, as a consequence of laziness and poor teaching, was doing great damage to the educational prospects of those being taught. To whom, if anyone, should she mention her very real anxieties? Was the likely damage to the possibilities of completing her third-year dissertation if she pursued her disquiet sufficient warrant to say nothing?

In both instances, the researchers were faced by moral qualms about how to act in the circumstances they confronted. They sought advice. Once moral debate is joined, all kinds of considerations crowd in upon us. Set on one side is always the weight to be attached to the research project and the importance of its pursuit in the life of the researcher. Sometimes we can persuade ourselves that what we hope to find out is so vital that in the moral 'equation' that has to be struck, potential research outcomes 'trump' moral considerations. Whether 'trumping' is plausibly on the cards will, of course, depend on just what the competing moral considerations are. No one, I suspect, would feel that intentionally killing a handful of people in pursuit of a striking medical breakthrough was, or could be, justified in the name of medicine. There might be greater acceptance of the same medical breakthrough on the basis of some minor inconvenience to individuals in cases where their consent was not sought.

However imprecise ways of talking in this area are, when it comes to 'balancing' or 'weighing' competing considerations against each other, there are judgements that characteristically we can share. There are others which we recognize that people like us (rational, good-willed, serious-minded, sensitive to the claims of morality upon us) can in good faith disagree about. What is truly disconcerting are those instances in which it is absolutely clear to us what ought to be done or felt, but we find others radically take moral issue with us or do not see an issue as a moral issue. The vast bulk of moral issues arising out of the conduct of social and educational research (surely) fall within that domain of issues that cater for disagreement between reasonable, well-intentioned individuals. What makes such debate so problematic is that the balancing of considerations is such a nice matter – there is no consideration or set of considerations that compel a particular moral outcome. If one of the parties to our debates simply did not see issues of consent as having any claim upon us, I am not sure how we could proceed to debate with that individual. Our discussion of moral issues associated with the conduct of research presumes a large measure of agreement about what is germane to our debates. We agree consent is an issue, we agree confidentiality should be respected, we agree we should ponder the outcomes of doing this rather than that, we agree we should do everything we can to avoid harming participants aiding our research, we agree children's interests should be protected, we do think privacy is important, we recognize our obligations to the wider research community, and so on. We can share a whole range of moral sentiments and attitudes, irrespective of how individually we would seek to vindicate such moral sentiments and attitudes. You might be a utilitarian, he looks to the authority of the Church, she sees reason as the arbiter of morality, I think morality is a mechanism for making things go better than otherwise they would between humans.

If advice is sought, the discussion that ensues can make explicit those dimensions of the debate that left to our own devices we might never think of, or to which we might not attach a proper importance. But we should not pander to the idea (flattering as it might be to those who sit on ethics committees at whatever level) that there are moral *experts* to whom we can appeal to divest ourselves of the responsibility for deciding what to do. Researchers bring to research themselves as individuals as well as the persona of social or educational researcher. In the latter guise, they have a primary obligation to the disinterested pursuit of truth. We have already noted that having truth as your taskmaster places its own moral constraints upon us. A serious commitment to truth rules out manipulating the evidence to achieve a preferred outcome, or to confirm a desired hypothesis. We noted that integrity is of the essence if our goal is truth. But truth, noble an ambition though it might be, is a non-moral ideal. Its achievement, of course, makes moral demands of us. Morality itself might be an arena of concern that has its own truths – though even if it is, our tragedy might be that we rarely know if we have found the true answer to a moral quandary. Be that as it may, human researchers dealing as they are with fellow humans cannot divest themselves of those moral obligations that should inform our dealings one with another.

Moral considerations are typically characterized as overriding considerations. This is normally thought to mean that if there is a conflict between moral and non-moral considerations, moral considerations, simply by virtue of being moral considerations, should prevail. The emphasis within all ethical codes of practice bearing upon social scientific and educational research upon key moral principles and concerns that should inform research practice largely reflects the sense that the unconstrained pursuit of truth is to be discouraged. Truth is to be ethically sought. The pursuit of truth has to be an ethical enterprise.

No one committed to the overriding status of morality in human affairs quite believes that *any* moral consideration overrides any non-moral consideration, whatever it might be. We are surely comfortable with the notion that, in the ethically-charged world of human research, on some occasions the quest for truth can outweigh the requirement of consent or the right to privacy (for example). What we cannot do is predict in advance the circumstances in which we would be justified in that judgement. I have already suggested that we all bring to our moral concerns a rather haphazard moral history, reflected in the principles, strong moral beliefs, sentiments and virtues that distinguish our individual moral outlooks. Moral decisions governing our conduct – and this is as true in social research as it is elsewhere – in order to be *moral*, decisions have to be our own. Once sensitive to an aspect of our research as raising a moral concern, it is entirely appropriate (if so minded) to seek advice from others. Talking things through may well help clarify in the mind of the researcher the issues to be addressed, and alert the researcher to aspects she might otherwise over-

Recommended Further Reading

If I had to recommend any one text to those wanting an illuminating overview of the issues and concerns defining 'the ethics of social research', it would be Roger Homan's *The Ethics of Social Research* (Longmans, 1991). Everyone, no matter at what stage of their career as researcher, could only read it with advantage. The discussion is grounded in an enviable familiarity with research literature and reports. It is a highly accessible text that does justice to its subject matter.

There is a challenging series of papers in the slightly earlier set of edited readings *Social Research Ethics: An Examination of the Merits of Covert Participant Observation*, Martin Bulmer (MacMillan, 1982). The entire collection comes highly recommended.

Joan E. Seiber's *Planning Ethically Responsible Research* (Sage, 1992) is a very useful guide on how to ensure the principles of ethical research are 'operationalized', as it were.

Partly reflecting my own predilections, some might find it interesting to look at a recent set of papers: *The Ethics of*

Educational Research, edited by M. McNamee and D. Bridges (Blackwell, 2002). They are of slightly variable quality but they represent a good example of what can happen when philosophers get their teeth into things. Whether they are likely to aid the researcher wrestling with a moral issue arising from a research project is a different matter.